WRITING ESSAYS

A Step-By-Step Instructional Guide for Middle and High Schoolers

By Late November Learning Tree

Late November

WRITING ESSAYS
A Step-By-Step Instructional Guide for Middle and High Schoolers
BY LATE NOVEMBER LEARNING TREE

Published by Late November Literary
Winston Salem, NC 27107

ISBN: 979-8-9892723-3-4

This is a work of nonfiction. Any brand names, places, or trademarks remain the property of their respective owners and are only used for educational purposes.

Library of Congress Cataloging-in-Publication Data:
Late November Learning Tree.
Writing Essays / Late November Learning Tree 1st ed.

Printed in the United States of America

Table of Contents

The Nuts and Bolts of Writing Essays 1

1: Essays Matter 3

2: The Traditional Essay 6

3: The Essay's Road Map 12

4: Practice Means Process 15

Practice Session: Making Strong Paragraphs 21

Mini-Essay #1: Reflection 51

Mini-Essay #2: Summary & Response 59

Essay #1: Opinion Essay 65

Essay #2: Comparison Essay 75

Essay #3: Literature Response Essay 87

Essay #4: Persuasive Essay 99

Essay Grading: Rubrics 111

THE NUTS
AND
BOLTS OF
WRITING
ESSAYS

1
Essays Matter

Essays. Not exactly a favorite word among students.

Writing essays can be nerve-wracking for teens and can cause great anxiety. Students often feel that there are too many rules to follow, or they struggle with grasping an individual instructor's specifications for what constitutes a good, well-written essay. It can turn into a headache, resulting in lackluster writing and a lack of desire to improve the craft.

Why Write Essays?

This question often gets asked by teens and young adults. Another variation of this question is, "When are we ever going to write an essay other than in school?" These are great questions, and they have equally great answers.

So, why do we write essays?

Answer: To better communicate through proper organization of thought.

When are we ever going to write an essay other than in school?

Answer: Not very often, if at all. However, you will communicate daily, and you will need to organize your thoughts and present them in several settings. Essay writing is the practice of this thought organization.

The Power of Organized Thought

Think of conversation. Someone is talking with you, and there is a train of thought.

Hey, what'd you do today?
Oh, not much. I took Rex to the vet. That's about it.
Is he okay? He's such a sweet dog.
He's been limping lately, so we wanted to get him checked out.
Hopefully, the vet had some answers.
It turned out to be a splinter in his paw. He's fine now.
I'm glad to hear it!

There's normally a purpose to the conversation. These conversations, or discussions, are often organized and follow a pattern. Have you ever been involved in a conversation where the topic became side-tracked, and no one could remember what was originally discussed? This disorganized thought process can actually be frustrating to some because they want to get to the point of the conversation.

Enter essays.

Essays put that organization into written action. It's taking a thought, examining the thought, possibly researching the thought, and expounding upon the thought. Essays allow student writers to learn and practice the art of organized communication.

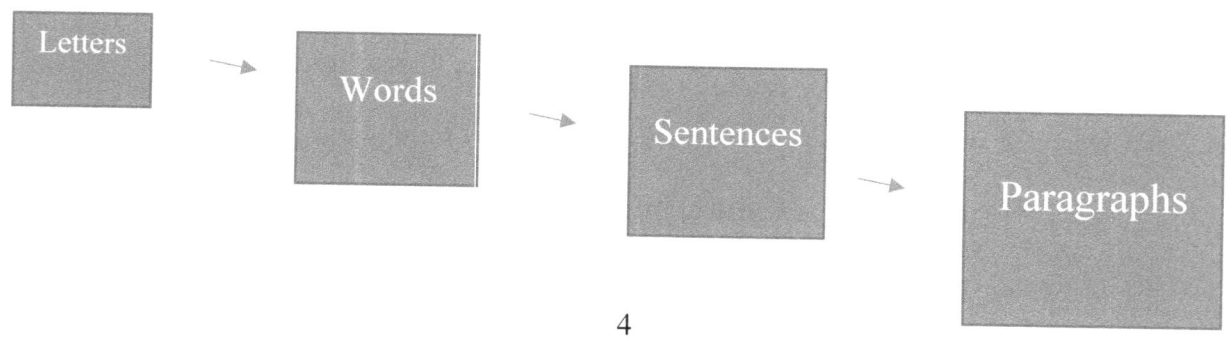

The Building Blocks of Language

The English language is often organized from the smallest component to the larger works. Think of written language. It starts with a letter, then we put those letters together to form a word. We then put words together in a strategic order to produce a sentence. Sentences, in turn, are often placed together in a train of thought known as a paragraph. Paragraphs are then brought together to form coherent essays or reports or books.

The essay is a natural step in the progression of students' learning experiences at the middle and high school levels. In their earlier years, they learned letters and sounds and how to put them together to form words. Each grade level progressed their knowledge of writing. When we explain this natural progression of written language, students have a better understanding of the importance of essays and other larger writing pieces. Essays do not have to be large. More on that later.

The important take-away is simply this: essays matter. Proper communication and organization of thought are necessities in today's global society. Now, let's figure out how to best write them.

2

The Traditional Essay

There are a variety of essays, but most follow a traditional structure. This traditional essay model is most often taught in secondary classrooms across the nation and is reinforced in college composition courses. It is simply known as the five-paragraph essay.

Broken down further, an essay has three crucial components: the introduction, the body, and the conclusion. Each of these parts have different requirements. Knowing the importance of each and what their requirements are will go a long way in helping your student learn and develop their essay writing skills. This workbook overall will focus on the traditional essay model.

The Introduction

The introduction is typically one paragraph. It's the first one of the essay, and it is arguably the most important paragraph. The introduction sets the stage for the rest of the essay. It hooks the reader, provides an overview of the essay topic, and ends with a thesis statement.

Components of the introduction paragraph:

➡ **Hook**

➡ **Overview of Topic**

➡ **Thesis Statement**

Organizing the introduction begins by hooking the reader into the topic. This is often called the attention grabber because the writer is grabbing the reader's attention. Hooks are often powerful quotes or significant statistics. Some hooks can even be a thought-provoking question. From there, the writer needs to provide an overview, which can be written in a variety of ways, depending on the type of essay being written. Some overviews may be a definition of the topic or may be informative sentences that provide statistics or important points about the topic. The hook and overview lead to the thesis statement, which states the specific topic of the essay.

Consider these sample introductions from a seventh-grade student, a ninth-grade student, and a twelfth-grade student:

Introduction #1 (seventh grade student):

Pandas, tigers, and whales. They need to be protected. Those are some who are almost gone. It's terrible, and we need to help them.

Introduction #2 (ninth grade student):

We need to protect endangered species. This is really important. There's lots of different animals that are nearly extinct, such as tigers and elephants. We need to stop hunting them and protect them instead.

> **Introduction #3 (twelfth grade student):**
>
> *Over two thousand animal species are listed as endangered, according to the Endangered Species Act. This list includes a variety of turtles, tigers, whales, and elephants, along with so many more. For an animal to be endangered, overhunting or loss of habitat threatens animal numbers. Humans can play a large part in this threat, especially when hunting for sport. Therefore, stricter hunting regulations need to be established and enforced to protect these endangered animals.*

These grade level samples show student work on the topic of endangered animals. It is evident that as students progress in their learning, their writing ability improves too. In each one of the examples, the students tried to create a compelling hook, provide an overview of endangered species, and state in the last sentence what the specific subject would be in the essay.

The Body

The body section of the traditional essay is much different than the introduction. Whereas the introduction introduces the topic to the reader and gives direction to what the essay will specifically discuss, the body paragraphs provide the information needed to best support the introduction. To accomplish this, body paragraphs require a different organizational technique.

The body paragraphs start with a topic sentence. This sentence should never be a quote, question, or specific example. Instead, a topic sentence is a statement of the main point of the paragraph. The rest of the paragraph simply supports the topic sentence. Here is a breakdown:

- A good body paragraph should be five-to-seven sentences long.
- A good body paragraph should focus on one topic.
- A good body paragraph should follow this pattern:
  - Topic Sentence
  - Supporting Sentence
  - Supporting Sentence
  - Supporting Sentence
  - Closing Sentence

Here are two body paragraphs on the topic of endangered species that follows the previous example introductions. See how each body paragraph focuses on a specific topic that each supports the main thesis of the essay.

Body Paragraph #1:

One reason to establish strict regulations to protect endangered wildlife is to protect the world's ecosystem. Everything has a place, and there is a certain balance to nature. When a species is eradicated, an imbalance can occur. Predators may lose substantial prey, or there may be an overabundance of critters because they no longer have natural predators. Divine design created ecosystem harmony, which means that every species has an important place in that design.

Body Paragraph #2:

Another reason that strict regulations are needed to protect endangered wildlife is that black market activity is dangerous and growing exponentially due to illegal poaching of these species. The black market happens around the world, and it buys and sells illegal animal products. For example, elephant tusks and white rhinoceros's body parts are being trafficked in these markets for high dollar, which makes illegal poaching a regularity. Black markets are international trafficking that is highly lucrative but extremely dangerous, pushing crime in various places. Endangered species are not safe in a world that sells their parts to the highest bidder.

The Conclusion

The conclusion paragraph is the last paragraph of the essay. Its job is to wrap up the key ideas and take-aways from the essay's content. It starts with a restated thesis, provides a summary of the key points, and leaves a strong final thought.

- The conclusion paragraph first restates the thesis.

- The conclusion paragraph summarizes the key points of the essay.

- The conclusion paragraph leaves the reader with a strong final thought.

The conclusion paragraph is often not as long as the other paragraphs, but that does not mean it is a weaker paragraph. It's succinct, but it's still powerful, strongly impacting the reader.

Conclusion Paragraph:

Establishing strict regulations to protect endangered species is humane and preserves our globe's ecosystems. Animals deserve to live in their natural habitats free from the terror of trophy hunting brought about by human greed. Without strict regulations, animal species will continue to go extinct at record rates. The divine may have given humans dominion over the animals, but that does not mean we should abuse that power.

Each of these essay components—the introduction paragraph, the body paragraphs, and the conclusion paragraph—have specific guidelines to help make the essay stand out and command attention. In the next chapter, we will discuss the importance of one single sentence in the essay, and that sentence is the thesis statement.

3

The Essay's Road Map

Every strong essay has a strong thesis statement. A thesis statement can sometimes be confusing to the student writer.

- What is a thesis statement?

- Where does it go?

- Is it required to have in an essay?

Think of the thesis statement as the essay's road map. Most of us do not enjoy taking a trip and getting lost along the way. It's disconcerting not to know where we are going. We feel more secure when we have clear direction. The same is true when reading an essay or report. When ideas are being thrown at the reader with little organization or when the reader is confused about where specifically the writer is taking them, most readers will set the writing down. We need clear direction as to the specific purpose for the essay and what we, as the readers, can expect.

This direction comes from the thesis statement. The thesis statement is in the introduction paragraph of an essay. Most teachers agree that the thesis statement is best placed as the last sentence in the introduction. This allows the writer to hook the reader and to provide an overview of the topic before giving the statement of direction (or thesis statement). Here is the introduction paragraph from the previous chapter. The thesis statement is underlined.

Introduction:

Over two thousand animal species are listed as endangered, according to the Endangered Species Act. This list includes a variety of turtles, tigers, whales, and elephants, along with so many more. For an animal to be endangered, overhunting or loss of habitat threatens animal numbers. Humans can play a large part in this threat, especially when hunting for sport. ***Therefore, stricter hunting regulations need to be established and enforced to protect these endangered animals.***

Thesis statements have specific rules that need to be followed.

1. Thesis statements are never statements of fact. Example: Night is written by Elie Weisel and is about his experiences as a teen enduring the Holocaust. This statement is true, and therefore, it doesn't qualify as a thesis statement.

2. Thesis statements are never questions. Example: What is your stand on abortion rights? Do you agree with me that abortion should be illegal? Thesis statements are meant to answer questions about what the essay is about. They are not to pose questions. Leave the questions for the opening of the essay.

3. Thesis statements make a statement that could be argued. They lead the reader into what the essay is about. They are clear statements of intent, stating the purpose of the essay.

An introductory way to think about thesis statements is to start a thesis statement this way: In this essay, I am going to discuss/explain… Eventually, a student needs to provide a strong statement without this introductory phrase, but it could be a good place to start for novice writers. See the example below.

Introduction (novice writer):

We need to protect endangered species. This is really important. There's lots of different animals that are nearly extinct, such as tigers and elephants. **In this paper, I will discuss how we need to stop hunting them and protect them instead.**

4

Practice Means Process

Good writing involves process. Part of what is so overwhelming to students is that the finished product is overwhelming to them. "You want me to write five paragraphs? About what? How am I going to do that?"

As stated earlier, writing is like building blocks. Process activities help us build the essay into more manageable sections. As you move through this workbook, it's important that you complete each process activity, which will help you write the best completed essay you can!

What are the steps to the writing process?

1. **Brainstorming**

2. **Outlining**

3. **Researching**

4. **Drafting**

5. **Revising and Editing**

6. **Publishing the Essay**

Process Step 1: Brainstorming

Brainstorming activities are a great way to get the student's brain to work on a topic. This is a much-needed activity for those who quibble that they don't know what to write. When we brainstorm, we come up with ideas, and we organize those ideas.

For example, let's say a student must write a research paper on the migration patterns of a specific bird. The student gets to pick which bird is going to be researched and written about.

- The student might participate in a discussion about possible birds to choose who have unique migration patterns.

- The student might be given a list of birds to research and write out a summary of their migration patterns.

- From there, the student might freewrite about a specific bird they found fascinating and come up with ideas that could work in a paper.

- The student could also use a mind-map to help organize different topic ideas and examples to include in each.

- The student might create a T-Chart to list how their specific bird species differ from other bird species.

Regardless of the essay's objective, brainstorming is a must. Each section in this workbook provides some brainstorming activity for the student to complete before they start outlining and drafting their essay. So, let's take a look at a couple of types of brainstorming activities.

Brainstorming: Freewrite

This is where you jot down any thoughts as they come to you about the topic. A freewrite doesn't worry about grammar or spelling or punctuation. The goal is to get the brain moving. For example, if the topic is endangered specifies in America, you would begin freewriting anything at all about endangered species. This is often the very first step to essay-writing. Most freewrites are uninterrupted brainstorming for 3 minutes.

Don't let your pencil leave the page. Just keep free flowing your thoughts about the topic.

_____

_____

_____

_____

_____

_____

_____

_____

_____

_____

_____

Brainstorming: Discussion with a Partner

Two heads are better than one! Many of us enjoy discussing a topic before we jump into writing about it. This activity involves finding another willing participant to discuss ideas and bounce them off each other.

Discussion Partner: _____

Potential Topic of Essay: _____

Questions to discuss with your partner:

What do we already know about the topic?

_____

_____

_____

What are your current feelings about the topic? Is it important to our world? Why or why not?

_____

_____

_____

If you could change one thing about this topic in the real world, what would it be and why?

_____

_____

_____

Why is raising awareness about this topic important? What should people know about it?

_____

_____

_____

If you were writing this essay, what would be the main take-away you'd want readers to have?

_____

_____

_____

Brainstorming: Q & A

This brainstorming activity works great for literature analysis or response essays. The question boxes help the student compartmentalize important information that could be helpful to include in the essay.

WHO?	WHAT?
WHEN?	**WHERE?**
HOW?	**WHY?**

Brainstorming: T-Chart

When it comes to opinion or persuasive essays, the T-Chart is an excellent brainstorming activity. One side of the "T" is to list the "pros" of an argument, and the other side is to list the "cons." Or, the left portion of the "T" lists reasons for an argument, and the right portion lists reasons against an argument. Some students also use the T-Chart for "agree" and "disagree" reasons on a specific topic.

REASONS *FOR* AN ARGUMENT "PROS"	REASONS *AGAINST* AN ARGUMENT "CONS"

Brainstorming: Mind-Map

In the center oval, students write the main topic of the essay. In the ovals surrounding it, students branch out into different categories of that topic. These make for good body paragraph ideas. Mind maps can be as simple or as complex as the student desires. They make a great visual of an essay's organization.

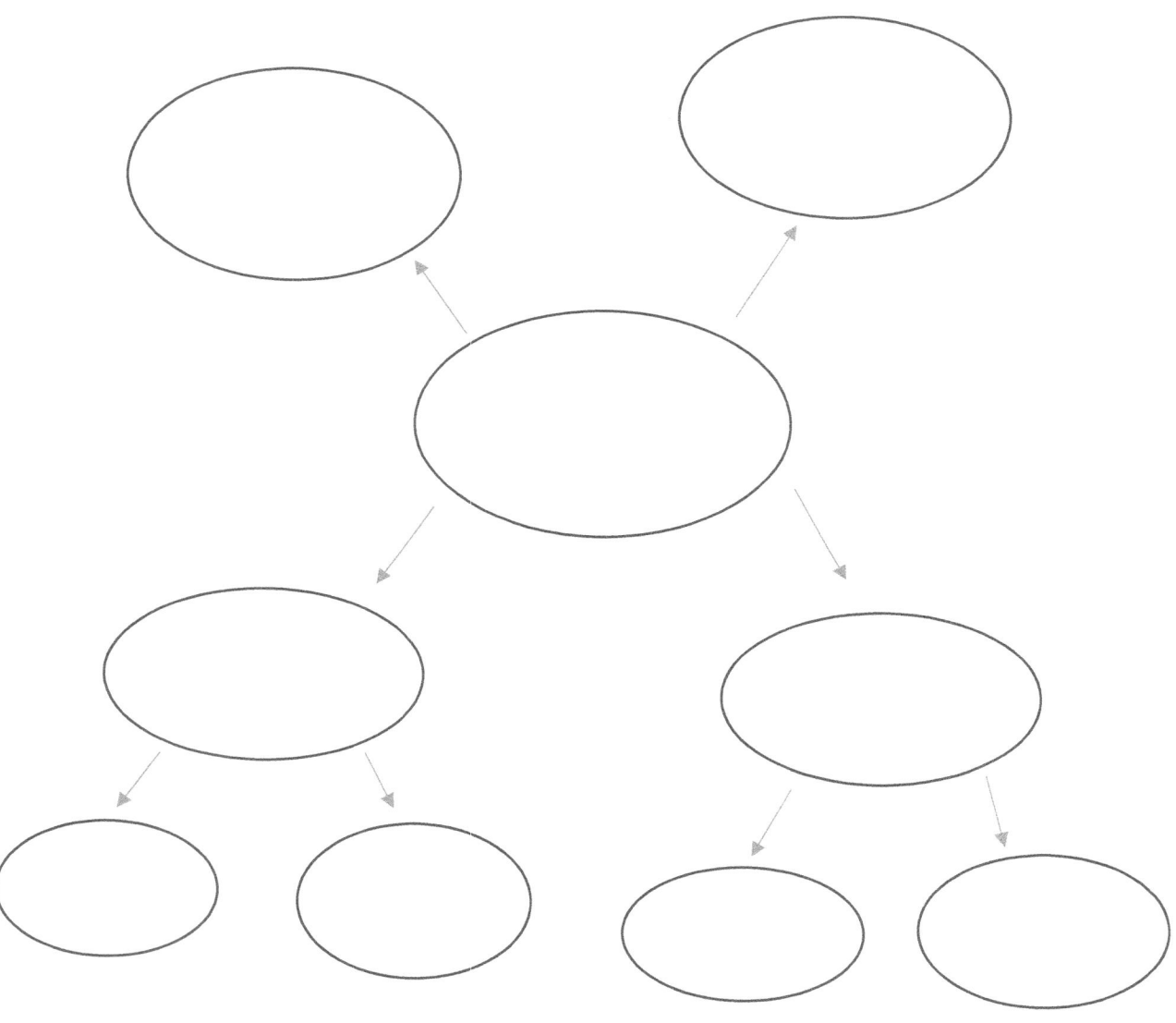

Process Step 2: Outlining

Once the student has an idea about what to write about, now comes the time to outline key points to be included in the essay. Some students like to skip outlining and jump right into drafting, but I caution against it. *Students may ask, "How do I write an outline?"*

Here's my response: Outlines are your friend! Don't know where to start when it comes to writing an essay? Start with an outline! An outline is like a skeleton of your essay. It allows you to write out a sentence or two in different sections to see how to best organize your thoughts.

Outlines often look like this:

I. **Introduction Paragraph**

    a. Attention Grabber (Hook)

    b. Overview of Topic

    c. Thesis Statement

II. **Body Paragraphs**

    a. Body Paragraph #1

    b. Body Paragraph #2

    c. Body Paragraph #3

III. **Conclusion Paragraph**

    a. Restated Thesis

    b. Summary of Key Points from Essay

    c. Final Thoughts

Process Steps 3 & 4: Researching & Drafting

Students should not jump right into a final, typed essay without the proper research and without writing a rough draft. Some essays do not necessarily require research, but some do.

Why Research?

- To support the assertions made in the essay.

- To provide a strong hook for the reader.

- To offer statistics and/or existing data to prove a point.

- To validate the writer's argument with supporting documentation.

- To add professional voices to the writer's voice through their own words via inserting of quotations.

When researching, it is important to document the author, title, source, and copyright in the writer's essay. This is accomplished through citations. There are several varieties of citation styles: APA, MLA, Chicago Manual, etc. Each of these provides their own rules for how and when to document sources.

Most Require a Two-Part Citation Process:

- In-text citation and…

- A bibliography or works cited list at the end of the essay.

For the purposes of this workbook, only a few essays require some research. Research worksheets are provided to assist in finding and recording documentation. It is up to the student to select which citation style to learn and incorporate into the essay.

Why Write a Rough Draft?

When it comes to writing an essay, teachers often require a rough draft. The reason for this is simple: writing is a process, and our first attempt at an essay should never be the final, published essay. This workbook breaks apart the draft into easy sections to help in the drafting process.

Introduction Paragraph:

_____

_____

_____

Body Paragraph #1:

_____

_____

_____

Body Paragraph #2:

_____

_____

_____

Body Paragraph #3:

_____

_____

_____

Conclusion Paragraph:

_____

_____

Process Steps 5 & 6: Revising, Editing, & Publishing

Now that the student's outline and draft are completed, there are important next steps.

1. A student should read his/her draft out loud. This will help the student catch any hiccups in his or her writing. A hiccup is where something doesn't read correctly when read out loud. It may be awkwardly worded, or there may be incorrect punctuation. Reading the draft out loud also helps to make sure the writing reads smoothly. If there needs to be corrections, the student should pause and make a note on the draft, so they don't forget to make the correction in the final copy.

2. A student should have someone else read the draft and help edit the document. This can be a peer, tutor, or teacher. A student should be open to the suggestions offered by the other individual and make corrections.

3. A student should take their revised and edited draft and type it up, following professional standards. *What does this mean?*

    a. An essay should be typed double-spaced.

    b. An essay should be in an easy-to-read font. Times New Roman and Arial are two popular fonts for essays.

    c. An essay should follow an essay format, which includes a centered title and left-aligned paragraphs that are indented.

4. Once typed, the student should print out a couple copies and have another reader or two take a critical look at the writing and point out any errors or confusing parts.

5. Make appropriate fixes one last time, and the student now has a professional, published essay!

Now that we understand essay writing is a process, let's get started with putting this process into practice. The rest of this workbook is divided into sections to help inspire writing and encourage specific processes to follow in writing essays.

- First, let's work on simple writing practices. These activities are simply writing two paragraphs that answer a specific prompt. This will help us become more comfortable with exploring our ideas and how to put them into paragraph form.

- After that, this workbook is broken down into different essay sections. Each section includes steps to the writing process: brainstorming, outlining, researching and drafting.

- By the end of this workbook, we will have written a reflection mini-essay, a summary and response mini-essay, an opinion essay, a comparison essay, a persuasive essay, and a literature response essay.

Are you ready? Let's roll up our sleeves and get writing!

PRACTICE SESSION:
MAKING STRONGER PARAGRAPHS

Practice Session: Making Strong Paragraphs

Paragraphs are written for a variety of different reasons (or purposes):

To inform

To persuade

To respond

To summarize

To clarify/explain

This week's paragraph work: To respond.

Responding to a prompt means explaining how both sides of the topic would respond. It is not an opinion response where you share your opinion.

Please write out two paragraphs that respond to this prompt:

Once they reach a certain age, parents should pay their children an allowance.

Example:

There are a lot of young people who probably feel that they deserve an allowance from their parents. They may think that they complete chores and help the family, so receiving some sort of payment only makes sense. Some chores that are most often performed by young people include taking out the trash, cleaning their rooms, or helping with the dishes and laundry. Providing an allowance for good work and fulfilling family responsibilities makes sense.

There are those who feel differently. They may argue that young people do not need an allowance. First, parents have household chores, and they don't receive any payment. It is about being a team. Each family member should contribute to the upkeep of their home because they all live there. Secondly, allowance sets up young people to feel entitled, which isn't helpful to them in the long run. Lastly, young people rarely complete chores without having an attitude or griping about the task. An allowance shouldn't be given when an attitude is present.

Your turn

Please write out two paragraphs that RESPOND to the prompt provided.

_____

_____

_____

_____

_____

_____

_____

_____

_____

_____

_____

_____

_____

_____

_____

_____

_____

_____

_____

_____

_____

_____

_____

_____

Practice Session: Making Strong Paragraphs

Paragraphs are written for a variety of different reasons (or purposes):

To inform

To persuade

To respond

To summarize

To clarify/explain

This week's paragraph work: To inform.

Please write out two paragraphs that inform the reader about a skill in which you are talented (Examples: singing, playing an instrument, writing, sports, cooking).

The purpose of these paragraphs is to inform the reader:

     (1) About the topic

     (2) Specific steps to complete the topic (or become better at it)

     (3) Potential challenges about the topic and/or ways to overcome those challenges.

Example:

     Thanksgiving is one of America's most favorite holidays, and cooking the best Thanksgiving meal is at the center of this important family holiday. My mother and I work hard to create the perfect family meal for this holiday, and I consider myself a true pro now. I have learned that to cook a Thanksgiving feast, one must be prepared. If a person waits until the last minute, she will become stressed, and the meal will not turn out well. The following paragraph will discuss the proper steps to put together this delicious holiday feast like a pro.

     There are proper steps to having a tasty Thanksgiving spread. First, make sure the turkey is thawed before the actual holiday. This means that it may need to be in the refrigerator for three-to-four days if it was purchased frozen. Another important step is to make the desserts a day or two before the holiday. This allows the cook to spend time on other items of the feast during the actual day. Before cooking the turkey, make sure to cook the sausage for the stuffing and mix those ingredients together. The bird needs to be stuffed before it begins roasting. Other food items, such as mashed potatoes and macaroni and cheese, can be cooked about an hour before mealtime. For a Thanksgiving feast to be successful, it is vital for success to give oneself enough time to complete the items without much overlap.

Your turn

Please write out two paragraphs that INFORM the reader about a skill in which you are talented.

_____

_____

_____

_____

_____

_____

_____

_____

_____

_____

_____

_____

_____

_____

_____

_____

_____

_____

Practice Session: Making Strong Paragraphs

Paragraphs are written for a variety of different reasons (or purposes):

To inform

To persuade

To respond

To summarize

To clarify/explain

This week's paragraph work: To clarify/explain.

The first paragraph provides clarity on the topic, and the second paragraph explains the reasons for the topic.

Please write out two paragraphs that provide clarification/explanation to this prompt:

Teens and their parents may not see eye-to-eye on important issues.

Example:

      Teens and parents sometimes struggle to see eye-to-eye on a variety of issues. For example, teens are often ready for their own cell phone at young ages, but they are often told no because their parents don't feel they need them. They may want to stay up late and sleep in, but parents wake up early and don't want their teens to sleep the day away. Sometimes teens and parents even differ when it comes to religious beliefs or political leanings.

      There is more than one reason for these differences. First, parents are of a different generation. They grew up without cell phones, so it's not a big deal to them not to have one. Or, they are trying to protect their children and teens, even if their children don't understand. Ultimately, adults try to teach children how to be responsible and respectful and that means not always getting what you want. Teens are learning about themselves and the world, and sometimes they want to branch away from their parents just to be different. The key is to make sure that love is always present in the relationship.

Your turn

Please write out two paragraphs that offer clarification/explanation to the prompt provided.

Practice Session: Making Strong Paragraphs

Paragraphs are written for a variety of different reasons (or purposes):

To inform

To persuade

To respond

To summarize

To clarify/explain

This week's paragraph work: To persuade.

Persuading is more than sharing an opinion. It provides strong examples as to why someone should agree with the writer. The goal is to persuade the reader to see the topic your way. This means providing strong examples to support your argument.

Please write out two paragraphs that respond to this prompt:

Should children/young people have electronic devices (televisions, computers, phones) in their bedrooms?

Example:

There are many reasons why young people should not have electronic devices in their rooms. First, there are a lot of questionable websites and games available online. When the devices are in the children's rooms, it is hard for parents to know what their children are watching or listening to. Furthermore, when all the entertainment is within the bedroom, it stops family connection. Family members will go to their rooms and shut their doors.

Electronic devices are best for everyone when they are in open spaces in the house. This way, the family can at least be in close proximity to each other. There is bound to be more interaction, which is good. Also, it prevents the temptation to click on websites that aren't appropriate. For these reasons, young people should avoid having electronic devices in their bedrooms.

Your turn

Please write out two paragraphs that PERSUADE the reader whether young people should be allowed electronic devices in their bedrooms.

Practice Session: Making Strong Paragraphs

Paragraphs are written for a variety of different reasons (or purposes):

To inform

To persuade

To respond

To summarize

To clarify/explain

This week's paragraph work: To summarize.

Summarizing provides an overview of a topic. It avoids giving an opinion. It simply offers organized information in a clear manner.

Please write out two paragraphs that summarize your favorite book or movie.

Example:

      Cinderella is a classic fairytale. In the story, it starts with a young girl orphaned and left to live with her stepmother and stepsisters. The stepmother is jealous of Cinderella's kindness and beauty and makes her a servant in her own home. As the years pass, this doesn't change Cinderella's personality, and she remains gentle and kind. When the family receives an invitation to a royal ball, Cinderella is excited that the invitation extends to her too. The stepmother and stepsisters have other ideas, and they busy Cinderella so that she is unable to prepare herself for the ball. After her stepfamily leaves, Cinderella is in tears until she meets her fairy godmother who grants her wish to attend the ball. She is given everything she needs to have a magical evening, but she is warned that when the clock strikes midnight, the spell will be broken, and everything will go back to the way it was.

      Cinderella has a grand time at the ball. She meets and dances with the prince throughout the evening. When she hears the clock strike midnight, she hurries away, leaving a glass slipper behind. While Cinderella goes back to her everyday life, the prince is determined to find the girl and marry her. The proclamation goes out that whichever girl fits the dainty glass slipper will meet and marry the prince. Even though the stepmother tries to stop the fateful meeting between Cinderella and the prince, she is no match for fate. Cinderella fits the glass slipper, and she and the prince get married.

Your turn

Please write out two paragraphs that SUMMARIZE your favorite book or movie.

_____

_____

_____

_____

_____

_____

_____

_____

_____

_____

_____

_____

_____

_____

_____

_____

_____

_____

_____

_____

_____

_____

_____

_____

_____

Practice Session: Making Strong Paragraphs

Paragraphs are written for a variety of different reasons (or purposes):

To inform

To persuade

To respond

To summarize

To clarify/explain

This week's paragraph work: To inform.

Please write out two paragraphs that inform the readers on the topic of animal habitats (you may need to research before writing your paragraphs):

Choose an animal or species of animal and write two paragraphs that inform the readers on the animal habitats.

(Example habitats: Do they live in the desert? Do they live in burrows? Do they live isolated or with their families?)

Example:

      Penguins are fascinating creatures and need specific habitats to survive. Most people know that penguins live in cold places like Antarctica, but they can also live in other regions and climates too. For example, penguins have been spotted on the shores of South Africa! Since penguins cannot fly but are excellent swimmers, they like to live in habitats where land predators are minimal and where they can be close to large bodies of water.

      Penguins also live in proximity with each other. There is safety in numbers not just in protection from predators but also to stay warm and protected from the elements. Penguins are family birds and will often stay with one mate for their entire lifespan. This creates a strong bond within their family unit.

Your turn

Please write out two paragraphs that INFORM the reader about an animal's habitat.

_____

_____

_____

_____

_____

_____

_____

_____

_____

_____

_____

_____

_____

_____

_____

_____

_____

_____

_____

_____

_____

_____

_____

_____

_____

Practice Session: Making Strong Paragraphs

Paragraphs are written for a variety of different reasons (or purposes):

To inform

To persuade

To respond

To summarize

To clarify/explain

This week's paragraph work: To persuade.

Please write out two paragraphs that persuade the reader:

Should college education be free?

Example:

There are many reasons why some may argue that college education should be free; however, the reality is that there are costs involved that someone must pay. Colleges do receive some subsidies and grants from government agencies, but the majority of their operating costs are paid for by student tuition. If tuition is no longer required for students to pay, an enormous challenge will occur. Colleges will be faced with billions of dollars in deficit.

Another important reason why college educations must have some cost is that it creates healthy competition between them and other industries. It is human nature to appreciate what we invest in. If something is handed to us, then we struggle to appreciate its value. A college education is a great resource, and all of these institutions offer scholarships and ways to earn an education while other industries promote other benefits they offer. Overall, it creates a strong market for employment when young adults have choices in their career paths. For these reasons, college education must cost something.

Your turn

Please write out two paragraphs that PERSUADE the reader whether college education should be free.

_____

_____

_____

_____

_____

_____

_____

_____

_____

_____

_____

_____

_____

_____

_____

_____

_____

_____

_____

_____

_____

Practice Session: Making Strong Paragraphs

Paragraphs are written for a variety of different reasons (or purposes):

To inform

To persuade

To respond

To summarize

To clarify/explain

This week's paragraph work: To respond.

Please write out two paragraphs that respond to this prompt:

Many view teens as lazy.

Example:

     Many view teens as lazy for several reasons. First, teens like to sleep in, and they don't like being told what to do. This may be perceived as lazy. Also, they are easily distracted and would rather chat with friends or flip through their phones than get their work done. Being with family and completing household chores probably ranks highest as their least favorite things to do, so they step back and refuse to participate. This can also be seen as lazy or, even worse, disrespectful.

     There are those who feel that teens are not lazy, but they are merely growing up and learning about the world around them. They are not fully adults, yet they are often expected to make adult decisions and complete adult tasks under the umbrella of "responsibility." When we consider that teens attend school five days a week and work after-school jobs, we can see that teens are not lazy. When teens are motivated, they truly accomplish great tasks, but they are particular about what motivates them.

Your turn

Please write out two paragraphs that RESPOND to the prompt that teens are lazy.

Practice Session: Making Strong Paragraphs

Paragraphs are written for a variety of different reasons (or purposes):

To inform

To persuade

To respond

To summarize

To clarify/explain

This week's paragraph work: To clarify/explain.

Remember that the first paragraph clarifies the topic by bringing awareness as to its truth. The second paragraph explains why it is perceived the way it is and what can be done to solve any challenge that comes from it.

Please write out two paragraphs that respond to this prompt:

Video games are often misunderstood and vilified.

Example:

Video games sometimes get a bad rap. They involve a lot of sitting and focused game play. There are times when gamers get upset or excited, and they may raise their voice. There are times when aggressive behavior occurs, and gamers throw their controllers or, even worse, punch a wall. Video games also get a bad reputation for keeping gamers from their families. Gamers will play with headsets on, which blocks outside noise, so there is no communication happening with those in close proximity because they are focused on hearing and responding to those who are involved in the game play.

One major explanation as to why video games are misunderstood or even vilified has to do with differing generations. Our parents and grandparents were raised in different generations when video games were not such a viable industry. Another explanation is that parents struggle to control the gaming activity because they often can't hear or participate in the game play. It also doesn't help that games are sometimes inappropriate for younger players, but parents are pressured to purchase the popular games anyway. Video games may be misunderstood, but parents can overcome these challenges and take a more active role in the game play of their children.

Your turn

Please write out two paragraphs that CLARIFY/EXPLAIN why video games are misunderstood.

_____

_____

_____

_____

_____

_____

_____

_____

_____

_____

_____

_____

_____

_____

_____

_____

_____

_____

_____

_____

_____

_____

_____

Practice Session: Making Strong Paragraphs

Paragraphs are written for a variety of different reasons (or purposes):

To inform

To persuade

To respond

To summarize

To clarify/explain

This week's paragraph work: To summarize.

Please write out two paragraphs that respond to this prompt:

Summarize the series of events of an important day in your life.

Example:

     I have worked hard to earn a black belt in taekwondo, so when the day arrived for it to happen, I was so excited. It took years for me to earn all the belts in the sport, and when I began working on the black belt moves, the intensity increased. I woke up on the day of my black belt test and after eating some breakfast I began to practice my moves. I watched videos provided to make sure my stand and movements were accurate and tried again.

     The afternoon came, and with it, my cousins and grandparents arrived. All my family wanted to be there to see me earn the black belt. We traveled to the martial arts center, and I left my family to take my place in the order of those testing. When the time came, I demonstrated several different Poomsae's, focusing on getting each position perfect. My instructor then directed me to perform a variety of kicks and punches. I also had to wait while other young people tested for their black belts. Soon, the time came when the instructor announced those who passed the black belt test. When my name was called, my family cheered, and I felt such a sense of accomplishment. That was an important day in my life, and I will never forget it.

Your turn

Please write out two paragraphs that SUMMARIZE an important series of events in your life.

_____

_____

_____

_____

_____

_____

_____

_____

_____

_____

_____

_____

_____

_____

_____

_____

_____

_____

_____

_____

_____

_____

_____

_____

MINI-ESSAY #1: REFLECTION

Reflection Mini-Essay

Directions:

Please write a four-paragraph essay that includes the steps of the writing process (brainstorming, outlining, drafting, typing, and revising/editing).

The essay must consist of:

- A small introduction paragraph (3-4 sentences)
- Two body paragraphs (5-to-7 sentences each)
- A small conclusion paragraph (3 sentences).
- Your final product will need to be typed and edited.

This mini-essay addresses the topic: A valuable learning experience

Some say that life is realizing that there is so much to learn. Please describe a valuable learning experience that helped you grow in wisdom, character, and/or integrity. Valuable experiences include lessons learned, life-changing events, wisdom learned from a challenging circumstance, etc.

- **Paragraph #1: Introduction**

  This first paragraph provides the reader with a hook or attention grabber to start the reflection. Then it introduces the situation by providing an overview. Its last sentence shares the valuable learning experience that will be talked about in the mini-essay.

- **Paragraphs 2 & 3: Body Paragraphs**

  The first body paragraph is going to describe the lesson learned or event in detail. The next body paragraph will reflect on the circumstances and how you've changed and/or grew because of it.

- **Paragraph #4: Conclusion**

  The final paragraph reiterates the valuable learning experience and how it has and will shape the student's future.

Organizing Your Reflection with Outlining

Topic:

_____

_____

Outline:

I. Introduction

a. Attention Grabber:

_____

b. Overview of Valuable Lesson:

_____

_____

c. Thesis Statement (What Did the Lesson Teach You?):

_____

_____

II. Body Paragraphs

a. Body Paragraph #1 (Describe Your Valuable Lesson) Topic Sentence:

_____

b. Body Paragraph #2 (Reflect on How You Changed & Grew from it) Topic Sentence:

_____

III. Conclusion

a. Restated Thesis (Restate the lesson learned):

_____

b. Closing Thoughts (How Will You Apply Lesson for Future):

_____

Introduction Paragraph Development
Of Reflection

Remember:

• Introductions are the first paragraph of the essay.

• Introductions start with an attention grabber (or hook).

• Introductions end with a thesis statement that states what valuable lesson you learned.

Introduction Paragraph:

_____

_____

_____

_____

_____

_____

_____

Body Paragraph(s) Development
Of Reflection

Remember:

• Body paragraphs are different than the introduction.

• Body paragraphs start with a topic sentence.

• Body paragraphs support the thesis statement.

Body Paragraph #1:

_____

_____

_____

_____

_____

_____

Body Paragraph #2:

_____

_____

_____

_____

_____

_____

Additional Notes:

_____

_____

Conclusion Paragraph Development
Of Reflection

Remember:

• The conclusion paragraph is different than the body and introduction.

• The conclusion paragraph starts by restating the thesis.

• The conclusion paragraph wraps up by emphasizing the topic's importance/relevance.

Conclusion:

_____

_____

_____

_____

_____

_____

_____

Sample Reflection Mini-Essay

Have you ever done something you regretted? Most of us have, but if we learn from it, we can grow and not repeat it. From the outside, it may look like I don't lead the most exciting life, so what regrets could I possibly have? I don't have many, but I do have one regret that taught me a valuable lesson. By being careless with my stuff, I hurt my sister. Several stitches later, my sister is fine, and a valuable lesson was learned.

My valuable lesson started on our family's little farm. My sister and I have chores, and one of them is to feed and take care of our chickens. We have a little area inside the barn for our supplies. It is where we store feed and different equipment. One major rule is to make sure we put all farm equipment back in its place. One morning I was in a hurry, and I was annoyed that my sister was taking her sweet time to get ready for school. I ran to where we keep our supplies, grabbed the bucket, filled it with feed, and hurriedly fed the chickens. I left the bucket out by the chicken fence, telling myself that my sister can put it back. She came out later and didn't see the bucket on the ground. She tripped over it, lost her balance, and hit her head against the fence. It sliced her head open, and she came screaming into the house, blood all over her face. She needed nine stitches.

The incident made me feel guilty and full of regret. I knew to put the bucket back, but I thought my sister could do it. I didn't think she'd be distracted and not see it. If I had followed the rules of our household and just put the bucket back with the supplies, my sister wouldn't have tripped, and she wouldn't have needed stitches. This valuable lesson taught me the importance of order and rules. Sometimes we think a rule or procedure is silly or that it doesn't always have to be followed, but from my experience, rules are meant to keep order, which is a good thing.

Overall, putting things back where they belong is a simple rule, and following it helps keep items where they belong, which also keeps people safe. I can't go back in time to fix my mistake, but I can learn from it. Thankfully, my sister is okay. She will have a scar the rest of her life, and I will always have the valuable lesson of following rules, especially putting things back where they belong.

MINI-ESSAY #2: SUMMARY & RESPONSE

Summary & Response

Mini-Essay Directions:

The Summary & Response is a four-paragraph essay that includes an introduction paragraph, two body paragraphs, and a conclusion paragraph.

1. Please find and read an article about a current event.

2. Please write out a summary of the article's main points (first body paragraph).

3. Please write out a response to the article's main points (second body paragraph).

Which article did you choose? _____

Who is the author? _____

What source/website did you find the article? _____

Summarize article here:

_____

_____

_____

_____

_____

Your Overall Response (Do you agree/disagree with the topic? What solutions can you come up with about the topic?):

_____

_____

_____

_____

_____

Summary & Response
Outline

Article Title and Author:

_____

_____

I. Introduction

a. Attention Grabber:

_____

b. Summary of Article:

_____

_____

c. Thesis Statement (Your Response):

_____

_____

II. Body Paragraphs

a. Body Paragraph #1: (Point #1 that you agreed or disagreed with)

_____

b. Body Paragraph #2: (Point #2 that you agreed or disagreed with)

_____

III. Conclusion

a. Restated Thesis:

_____

b. Closing Thoughts (Your Overall Response to the Article):

_____

_____

Summary & Response Essay
Rough Draft

Introduction Paragraph:

_____

_____

_____

_____

Body Paragraph #1:

_____

_____

_____

_____

Body Paragraph #2:

_____

_____

_____

_____

Conclusion:

_____

_____

_____

_____

Sample Summary & Response Essay

Should schools ban cell phones? According to the article, "Schools Don't Want Kids on Cell Phones," by Alia Wong and Nirvi Shah, many schools are opting to ban cell phone use during the school day. School officials reasoned that students were too distracted by the phones and that cell phone use increased bullying on campus. Some students and parents argued that banning cell phones was going too far. Overall, the article listed many solid reasons why cell phones should be banned, and after consideration, I agree with the article.

One of the main points the article discusses is that students are distracted by their phones. I see this first-hand. Students are so busy looking at their phones that they are not paying attention in class. They also text each other, which then distracts their friends. Even for students trying to do their work, the constant buzzing or ringtones from phones is distracting. Not having phones in the classrooms would help us focus more on the teacher and completing our assignments.

Another main point of the article is that students like to record violence or other inappropriate content that might take place during the school day. This is definitely a valid point because there are a lot of popular social media apps that students post videos to throughout the day. This increases bullying, and it increases misbehavior with teachers because students want the views or likes.

The authors made valid points in their article, "Schools Don't Want Kids on Cell Phones," and I agree with most of them. Students do like their cell phones, but they are distracting and can promote bullying. My suggestion is to allow cell phones during lunch but not during class time. No matter what, students should respect whatever rule their school administrators enforce.

1:
ESSAYS
MATTER

Everyone has opinions! So, let's start here.

For our first full-length essay, we will be writing an opinion essay. Below is a list of topics that you can use for this essay. You want to pick a topic that you have an opinion about. This means you strongly feel one way or another. Is there a topic you'd like to write about that's not on the list? No problem! You can choose whatever topic works for you.

Good Topics for an Opinion Essay:

1. What is your opinion about eating vegetables?

2. What is your opinion about curfews and bedtimes?

3. What is your opinion about required gym classes?

4. What is your opinion about children and cell phones?

5. What is your opinion about parental controls on television shows and movies?

6. What is your opinion about the best restaurant/food item in the world?

7. What is your opinion about the best sport/sports team in the world?

8. What is your opinion about the best vacation a person could ever take?

9. What is your opinion about the best video game/board game?

10. What is your opinion on vaccinations?

11. What is your opinion about homeschooling?

12. What is your opinion about the importance of going to college or trade school?

13. What is your opinion about the importance of family?

14. What is your opinion on what to do to help those in need?

What topic did you select? _____

Opinion Essay
Outline

I. Introduction

a. Attention Grabber (hook the reader with a strong question or fact about the topic):

_____

b. Overview of Topic:

_____

_____

c. Thesis Statement (What is the general statement of your opinion on the topic):

_____

_____

II. Body Paragraphs

a. Body Paragraph #1: The first reason why your opinion is valid.

_____

b. Body Paragraph #2: The second reason why your opinion is valid.

_____

c. Body Paragraph #3: The third reason why your opinion is valid.

_____

III. Conclusion

a. Restated Thesis:

_____

b. Closing Thoughts (Summary of your reasons for your opinion on the topic):

_____

_____

Introduction Paragraph of Opinion Essay:

Hook (How are you going to grab the reader's attention? Try a question or a statistic about your topic):

_____

_____

Overview of Topic (provide general information about the topic; this will lead to the thesis):

_____

_____

Thesis Statement (What is your essay going to be about? This is where you provide direction to the reader about what they will learn in your essay):

_____

_____

Now, put it all together in a complete introduction paragraph. Read it out loud to make sure it reads well and flows smoothly. Fix any errors.

_____

_____

_____

_____

_____

_____

Body Paragraphs of Opinion Essay:

Body Paragraph #1: Let's start with the most important point you would like to make in your paper. The first body paragraph should be your strongest idea. Make sure you have a strong topic sentence followed by supporting sentences and examples to that topic sentence. Read it out loud to make sure it reads well and flows smoothly. Fix any errors.

_____

_____

_____

_____

_____

_____

_____

_____

Body Paragraph #2: This is for the second most important point you would like to make in your paper. This paragraph should be just as strong as the first body paragraph. Make sure you have a strong topic sentence followed by supporting sentences and examples to that topic sentence. Read it out loud to make sure it reads well and flows smoothly. Fix any errors.

_____

_____

_____

_____

_____

_____

_____

Body Paragraph #3: This is the third important point you would like to make. It should be just as strong as the first two body paragraphs. Make sure you have a strong topic sentence followed by supporting sentences and examples to that topic sentence. Read it out loud to make sure it reads well and flows smoothly. Fix any errors.

_____

_____

_____

_____

_____

_____

_____

_____

Conclusion Paragraph of Opinion Essay:

Restated Thesis (This is a general statement reminding the reader of the focus of the essay):

_____

_____

Review of Essay's Topic (provide the main points of the essay):

_____

_____

_____

Final Thoughts (This is where you, as the author, leave the reader with strong, thought-provoking statements):

_____

_____

_____

Now, put it all together in a complete conclusion paragraph. Read it out loud to make sure it reads well and flows smoothly. Fix any errors.

_____

_____

_____

_____

_____

_____

_____

Sample Opinion Essay:

What is the best sport in all the world? This is a tough question because there are a lot of sports to choose from: American football, global soccer, basketball, hockey, golf, volleyball, baseball, tennis, etc. Most sports focus on a specific skill and set of rules, but they vary on their objectives. One sport that often gets overlooked is cheerleading. Cheerleading demands physical fitness, teamwork, and in my opinion, it is the best sport in the world.

First, cheerleading is the best sport because it pushes participants to be in their top physical health. Cheerleading involves rigorous dance routines, specific movements, lifting of other cheerleaders, and often, catching of cheerleaders. This cannot be done without strength, resilience, and much practice. If someone wants to join a sport that is going to push them to be in the best physical shape, then cheerleading is a viable contender.

Second, cheerleading is the best sport because it requires teamwork from all participants. All routines—whether chants or dance—require choreography and every team member must know their part down to the second. Cheerleaders must trust each other to lift one another up, as well as to catch them when the routine calls for it. For these reasons, the bond between cheerleaders is often quite strong.

Lastly, cheerleading is the best sport because its main goal is to encourage other sports teams within their programs, as well as the fans and spectators in the audience. With cheerleading, attitude is everything because others are counting on the cheerleader to cheer, dance, shout, and stay positive regardless of how the other teams are playing. Cheerleaders must push past discouragement and keep a smile on their face. This positivity is contagious and spreads throughout games and competitions.

There may be a lot of sports, but cheerleading is definitely a top contender for the best sport in the world. No other sport focuses on encouraging other teams and those in the crowd to stay hyped and positive during a match. It may not garner the same number of fans or generate the same profits as other sports, but cheerleading is not for the faint of heart.

2: THE TRADITIONAL ESSAY

Comparison

Essay Directions

Directions:

Please write a five-paragraph essay that includes the steps of the writing process (brainstorming, outlining, drafting, typing, and revising/editing). The essay must consist of an introduction paragraph, three body paragraphs, and a conclusion paragraph. Your final product will need to be typed and edited.

Some research is required.

This essay is an informative essay that will *compare and contrast* **two associated topics, highlighting the similarities and differences between them.**

Sample Topics:

1. One religion versus another religion (Christianity vs. Buddhism).

2. Homeschooling versus Traditional Schooling.

3. Predator versus predator (Sharks versus wolves).

4. One restaurant versus another restaurant (or eating out versus eating at home).

5. One country versus another country (U.S.A. versus China).

6. A topic of your choosing (please get it approved by instructor).

Comparison Brainstorm Activities

Freewrite:

What topic(s) are interesting to you that could make a good essay? Write out what you know about these topics and/or what you would like to learn about these topics. How do they compare/relate to each other?

_____

_____

_____

_____

_____

_____

_____

_____

_____

_____

Brainstorm: List what you already know about the two topics and/or what you'd like to know.

Topic 1 Ideas:	Topic 2 Ideas:
1.	1.
2.	2.
3.	3.
4.	4.
5.	5.
6.	6.
7.	7.

Research Worksheet for Comparison Essay

What is your first source? Write out complete citation (Author's name, "Title," Source, Copyright, URL):

_____

_____

_____

What information from the source do you plan to use? (There should possibly be STATISTICS or important information to your topic or strong quotes to support your assertions):

_____

_____

_____

_____

_____

_____

_____

What is your second source? Write out complete citation (Author's name, "Title," Source, Copyright, URL):

_____

_____

_____

What information from the source do you plan to use? (There should possibly be STATISTICS or important information to your topic or strong quotes to support your assertions):

_____

_____

_____

_____

_____

_____

Comparison Sample Outline

Sample Outline (Read through this before you start your own):

I. Introduction

a. Hook:

For millions of young adults, the college experience is something they desire (SOURCE).

b. Summary of both topics (provide brief overview of each):

Some young adults choose colleges close to home because of convenience and cost effectiveness. Other young adults desire the complete college experience offered at universities around the country.

c. Thesis: (Similarities and Differences that will be discussed):

This paper is going to compare community colleges versus universities.

II. Body Paragraphs

a. Similarity/Difference #1:

The first similarity to be discussed is that they both provide college classes toward a degree.

b. Similarity/Difference #2:

A big difference is the college experience.

c. Similarity/Difference #3:

Lastly, I'm going to explore cost and how it's different between the two.

III. Conclusion

a. Restate Thesis:

This paper looked at how colleges are different, specifically community colleges and universities.

b. What is your final take-away on the topic(s)?

Some feel that universities offer a more complete college experience, and they are worth the investment. Others choose the community college because it is affordable and close to home. Whatever decision families choose, it is important to research and know the pros an cons of each of these selections.

Comparison Outline

I. Introduction:

a. Hook:

_____

_____(Source).

b. Overview of two topics:

_____

_____

_____

c. Thesis:

_____

_____

II. Body Paragraphs

a. Similarity or Difference #1:

_____

b. Similarity or Difference #2:

_____

c. Similarity or Difference #3:

_____

III. Conclusion

a. Restated Thesis:

_____

_____

b. Final Take-aways:

_____

_____

Comparison
Rough draft

Introduction: Hook, overview of both topics, strong thesis statement

_____

_____

_____

_____

_____

Body Paragraph #1: Similarity or Difference #1

_____

_____

_____

_____

_____

Body Paragraph #2: Similarity or Difference #2

_____

_____

_____

_____

Body Paragraph #3: Similarity or Difference #3

_____

_____

_____

_____

_____

Conclusion: Restate Thesis & Provide Take-Away of the two topics

_____

_____

_____

_____

_____

Sample Comparison Essay:

For millions of young adults, the college experience is something they desire (Smith, 2021). The reasons for this vary, but many high school graduates know that a college education is the gateway to their potential careers. Some young adults choose colleges close to home because of convenience and cost effectiveness. Other young adults desire the complete college experience offered at universities around the country. Both options have benefits and drawbacks, and the following paragraphs will compare community colleges and universities to help inform the reader.

One important benefit of both community colleges and universities is each of them provide college classes toward a degree. There are hundreds of college degrees to choose from, and both types of institutions have specific degree programs for a myriad of student interests. Community colleges often specialize in two-year degree programs and certifications while universities often offer four-year degrees and graduate studies. Some students choose to attend a community college to earn two years of general credits that easily transfer to a university. Others earn a two-year degree at the community college and are ready for the job market. For those desiring to extend their learning, universities are ready to accommodate.

A big difference between community colleges and universities is the college experience. Community colleges are within the same county as the student, which offers convenience and often peace of mind. These local schools do boast of some sports and clubs, but most students attend classes only, commuting instead of staying on campus. Universities promote their sports teams and activities and include on-campus accommodations for students to live there. This enhances the college experience and allows the students to connect to their peers and collegiate atmosphere in ways that a community college does not.

It is important to note the cost factor for each of these types of institutions. Community colleges are substantially more ccst effective and on average charge about $4000 per year ("How Much Is Community College," 2021). Some community colleges are now offering free tuition to students within the county who have recently graduated. On the other hand, university costs have skyrocketed, and on average, universities cost double in terms of tuition. To live on campus also comes with a hefty price tag, costing students between $20,000 to $30,000 annually for public institutions ("Tuition Costs of Colleges and Universities," 2022). Understanding how much each of these types of institutions cost is paramount before making a college decision.

All colleges are different, specifically community colleges and universities. Knowing the benefits and drawbacks for each is important before making a college decision. Some feel that universities offer a more complete college experience, and they are worth the investment. Others choose the community college because it is affordable and close to home. Whatever decision families choose, it is important to research and know the pros and cons of each of these selections.

ESSAY #3: LITERATURE RESPONSE ESSAY

Literature Response
Essay Directions

Directions:

Please write a five-paragraph essay literature response that includes the steps of the writing process (brainstorming, outlining, drafting, typing, and revising/editing). The essay must consist of an introduction paragraph, three body paragraphs, and a conclusion paragraph. Your final product will need to be typed and edited. *Reading of a text selection is required.*

This essay is a literature response assignment that explores the plot, characters, and key themes of a reading selection. For the sake of this assignment, we recommend the following classics. Choose one to read before completing the essay.

Middle Grade Novels:

1. *The Lion, the Witch, and the Wardrobe,* by C.S. Lewis
2. *A Wrinkle in Time,* by Madeleine L'Engle
3. *Matilda,* by Roald Dahl
4. *Because of Winn Dixie,* by Kate Dicamillo
5. *Homeless Bird,* by Gloria Whelan
6. *Number the Stars,* by Lois Lowry
7. *Hatchet,* by Gary Paulsen

High School Novels:

8. *To Kill a Mockingbird,* by Harper Lee
9. *Night,* by Elie Wiesel
10. *Fahrenheit 451,* by Ray Bradbury
11. *A Raisin in the Sun,* by Lorraine Hansberry
12. *Animal Farm,* by George Orwell
13. *The Lord of the Rings,* J.R.R. Tolkien
14. A book of your choosing

Step-By-Step Instructions:

1. **Read a book of your choosing** (See the list of recommended books from the list on the previous page). This can already be a book that is a part of your curriculum.

2. Once the book is completed, you are ready to get started on writing a literature response. *A literature response is when a reader discusses the main plot of the book, the characters that stood out, how the book made the reader feel, and the important themes—or life lessons—that the book imparted.*

3. **To begin a literature response, let's start with brainstorming:**

   a. **First, make a list of the important events that took place in the book.** You'll use this list later for your plot paragraph.

   b. **Second, make a list of the important characters and what you liked and/or didn't like about them.** Who was the protagonist (main character)? Who was the antagonist (the character causing a lot of the problems)? Is there a character that you really connected with? If so, make sure they make the list and write out why you connected with them!

   c. **Next, brainstorm the main themes of the book.** Themes are the main lessons learned or the key take-aways the reader has after reading it. Themes are not plot points, but they are overarching ideas and/or morals to be applied to the reader's life.

4. **Use your brainstorming lists to begin to construct a literature response essay.** A literature response essay examines and answers these questions:

   a. *What was the book about? What were the main plot points?*

   b. *What lessons learned by the characters also apply to the reader?*

   c. *How did the book make me feel as I was reading it? Why is that?*

   d. *Which character do I most connect with? Why is that?*

   e. *If I could change anything about the book, what would I change? Why?*

Literature Response Brainstorm Activities

Freewrite:

What did you like or not like about the book? Discuss the parts of the book that really stuck out to you, or if there was something that you would change about the book. Lastly, what lessons did the characters learn that could apply in your own life?

_____

_____

_____

_____

_____

_____

_____

_____

_____

Brainstorm: Plot Points

Write out a list of important events that took place in the novel. Add more to the list if needed.

1.

2.

3.

4.

5.

6.

7.

8.

9.

10.

11.

12.

91

Research Worksheet for Literature Response Essay

Write out the author's name, title of the book you read, and the copyright year (often located at the beginning pages of a novel):

_____

_____

Quote #1: Literature Response Essays are often stronger with quotes from the novel to support your main points. Find an important quote from your novel that you'd like to include in your essay:

_____

_____

_____

_____

Quote #2: Literature Response Essays are often stronger with quotes from the novel to support your main points. Find an important quote from your novel that you'd like to include in your essay:

_____

_____

_____

_____

Quote #3: Literature Response Essays are often stronger with quotes from the novel to support your main points. Find an important quote from your novel that you'd like to include in your essay:

_____

_____

_____

_____

Literature Response Outline

I. Introduction:

a. Hook:

_____

_____

b. Overview of the book (include title and author):

_____

_____

_____

c. Thesis:

_____

_____

II. Body Paragraphs

a. Body Paragraph #1 summarizes the important events of the book:

_____

b. Body Paragraph #2 examines the important character(s) and what they learned in the novel:

_____

c. Body Paragraph #3 discusses the main themes of the book that can apply to the reader:

_____

III. Conclusion

a. Restated Thesis:

_____

_____

b. Reader's Overall Response to the novel (was it positive or negative…please explain why):

_____

_____

Literature Response
Rough draft

Introduction: Hook, overview of novel and themes, strong thesis statement

_____

_____

_____

_____

_____

_____

Body Paragraph #1: Summary of Plot

_____

_____

_____

_____

_____

Body Paragraph #2: Examination of Characters

_____

_____

_____

_____

Body Paragraph #3: Main Themes from the Novel that Apply to the Reader

_____

_____

_____

_____

_____

_____

Conclusion: Restate Thesis & Provide Final Response to the Novel (positive or negative)

_____

_____

_____

_____

_____

_____

Sample Literature Response Essay:

"I wondered if Hari's parents were ashamed to admit...that they had married so young and so sick a son to get money," (Whelan, *Homeless Bird*). What would it be like to marry someone at the age of thirteen? In *Homeless Bird*, by Gloria Whelan, a girl named Koly is forced into an arranged marriage. Since this book takes place in India, this is the custom of Koly's family and village. Unfortunately, Koly's young husband is sickly and dies soon after their marriage, making her a widow living with her cruel mother-in-law. Koly is a relatable character who shows resilience and strength in the face of tragedy and abuse, and readers can learn a lot about her in Whelan's book.

Koly's faces many challenges throughout *Homeless Bird*. First, she must marry into a family whom she's never met. The boy she marries is named Hari, and he is sick with tuberculosis. The only reason his parents allowed the marriage was to take the money from Koly's dowry and pay for a trip into the holy city of Varanasi to dip in the Ganges River. Now Koly is stuck living with Hari and his family: his mean-spirited mother, who she refers to as Sass, his distant father, who she refers to as Sassur, and his younger sister, Chandra, who Koly draws close to after Hari's death. Unfortunately, not long after Hari's death, Chandra gets married off to an affluent man, leaving Koly alone with her in-laws. Sass's cruelty is throughout the novel. Then when Sassur dies, Sass abandons Koly. Koly becomes a homeless widow in a foreign city. It is in this strange city that she meets Raji, a poor rickshaw driver who becomes her friend. He takes her to a widow's house where she is provided for. Soon, with Raji's help, Koly overcomes the trials of life and begins to earn a living with her beautiful quilts.

Several characters add to the richness of this novel. The first one is Koly who is an empathetic protagonist. She faces many hardships in life, and the reader feels her pain throughout the novel. Then there is Sass who is the main antagonist. She is cruel, yet the reader is sympathetic to her plight because she loses her son to tuberculosis, then she loses her husband too. However, these deaths do not absolve her of wrongdoing, and in her, the reader learns what not to become. Lastly, there is the character of Raji who shows the reader what kindness and compassion look like. He helps Koly find a home when she's abandoned, and he also gives her love, which she never truly experienced before meeting him.

The main theme of *Homeless Bird* is no matter how hopeless life becomes never give up. When the worst of life happened to Koly, it still led her to Raji who showed her true love. Ultimately, the book reinforces that life may not always be fair, but it can still lead to beautiful beginnings and happy endings. The best thing that happened to Koly—Sass's abandoning her—didn't feel good when she was going through it, yet it needed to happen for her to meet the love of her life.

Homeless Bird captures the reader's heart with Koly's misadventures and eventual happiness. At first, this reader found the novel depressing. Koly had to endure a lot of negative circumstances. Sass's cruelty was sometimes hard to read. However, watching Koly find herself on the streets as a homeless widow and then meeting Raji was poetic justice. It was a reminder that beauty can bloom from ashes. Everyone should read this wonderful book.

ESSAY #4: PERSUASIVE ESSAY

Persuasive Essay
Directions

Directions:

Please write a five-paragraph essay that includes the steps of the writing process (brainstorming, outlining, drafting, typing, and revising/editing). The essay must consist of an introduction paragraph, three body paragraphs, and a conclusion paragraph. Your final product will need to be typed and edited.

Research is required.

This essay is a *persuasive essay*. In it, you will need to take a stand *for* or *against* an important topic in today's culture. You are then to persuade the reader through strong arguments in support of your stand on the topic.

Sample Topics:

1. For or Against Abortion

2. For or Against Creationism or Evolution Taught in Schools

3. For or Against the Banning of Tobacco Products in the U.S.

4. For or Against the Electoral College in America

5. For or Against the Fracking of Oil to Become More Energy Independent

6. For or Against Armed Security in Public Schools

7. For or Against Stricter Regulations on Gun Ownership

8. For or Against Animal Testing on Cosmetics

9. For or Against Radical Climate Change Initiatives

10. For or Against _____ (your choice)

Persuasive Essay Brainstorm Activities

Your Argument Topic: _____

REASONS *FOR* AN ARGUMENT "PROS"	REASONS *AGAINST* AN ARGUMENT "CONS"

Persuasive Essay
Example Outline

Topic: *What is sport hunting? Should it be banned?*

Introduction Paragraph:

The introduction is going to build the topic of hunting for sport. It will examine both sides, but it will need to end with a strong statement (thesis) supporting one side of the issue.

1. **Attention Grabber (Hook): (1-2 sentences that provide an interesting fact about the topic. This helps to "hook" the reader.)**

   Approximately 100,000 animals are killed each year because of sport hunting. This is not to be confused with the millions of animals killed each year for sustenance hunting (for food, animal hide, etc.).

2. **Overview of Topic: (2-3 sentences that provide a summary of the general topic. It often highlights different sides of a topic in an unbiased way)**

   Sport hunting is also called trophy hunting, and it is about killing animals for some sort of tangible prize or the simple exhilaration of being successful on a hunt. Some argue that sport hunting is cruel and serves no purpose. Others argue that sport hunting helps to control animal populations and is a great recreational activity.

3. **Thesis Statement: (1-2 sentences that provide a specific statement of the essay's stand on the topic)**

   Sport hunting will be further explained in the following paragraphs, along with reasons that it should be banned from all parts of the world.

Body Paragraphs:

Body Paragraphs will need to focus on key points that best support the thesis statement.

1. **Topic Sentence for Body Paragraph #1:**

   Sport hunting often revolves around endangered species with selling animal products in black market trades.

   Support and Examples follow the topic sentence.

103

2. **Topic Sentence for Body Paragraph #2:**

   Sport hunting has already eradicated many animal species from our planet.

   Support and examples follow the topic sentence.

3. **Topic Sentence for Body Paragraph #3:**

   Sport hunting carries a large price tag, and the money can be better served elsewhere.

   Support and examples follow the topic sentence.

Conclusion Paragraph:

The conclusion paragraph does not have to be a large paragraph. It simply restates what the essay was about and summarizes the key take-aways.

1. **Restated Thesis:** (1 sentence that captures the essence of the essay)

   There may be reasons for sport hunting to continue, but the reasons not to sport hunt far outweigh them.

2. **Closing Thoughts:**

   Taking care of God's creatures falls upon mankind, and hunting for nothing more than a trophy is killing for sport. With many of the big game now endangered, protecting them should be a priority.

Persuasive Essay Outline

I. Introduction:

a. Hook:

_____

_____

b. Overview of Topic:

_____

_____

_____

c. Thesis (Provide a Clear Stand on the Topic):

_____

_____

II. Body Paragraphs

a. Body Paragraph #1 is the first argument in support of the thesis:

_____

b. Body Paragraph #2 is the second argument in support of the thesis:

_____

c. Body Paragraph #3 is the third argument in support of the thesis:

_____

III. Conclusion

a. Restated Thesis:

_____

_____

b. Summary of Arguments in Support of Thesis:

_____

_____

Research Worksheet for Persuasive Essay

The Persuasive Essay should incorporate at least three professional sources to support your argument. This will require you to find articles online that provide strong context, definitions, and statistics that you can use to best support your argument. Use the following worksheet to document your source and the information you plan to use in the essay.

What is your first source? Write out complete citation (Author's name, "Title," Source, Copyright, URL):

_____

_____

_____

What information from the source do you plan to use? (There should possibly be STATISTICS or important information to your topic or strong quotes to support your assertions):

_____

_____

_____

_____

_____

_____

_____

What is your second source? Write out complete citation (Author's name, "Title," Source, Copyright, URL):

_____

_____

_____

What information from the source do you plan to use? (There should possibly be STATISTICS or important information to your topic or strong quotes to support your assertions):

_____

_____

_____

_____

_____

_____

What is your third source? Write out complete citation (Author's name, "Title," Source, Copyright, URL):

_____

_____

What information from the source do you plan to use? (There should possibly be STATISTICS or important information to your topic or strong quotes to support your assertions):

_____

_____

_____

_____

_____

_____

Persuasive Essay
Rough draft

Introduction: Hook, overview of topic, strong thesis statement that provides a stand on the topic that will be argued throughout the essay

_____

_____

_____

_____

_____

_____

Body Paragraph #1: Argument #1 in support of the thesis statement

_____

_____

_____

_____

_____

_____

Body Paragraph #2: Argument #2 in support of the thesis statement

_____

_____

_____

_____

Body Paragraph #3: Argument #3 in support of the thesis statement

Conclusion: Restate Thesis & Provide Summary of Arguments in Support of Thesis

ESSAY GRADING: RUBRICS

Basic Essay Rubric

Grading Categories	Excellent	Good (Some Improvement Needed)	Fair (Not Yet Proficient)
Content _____/20 pts.	Essay content is strong. There is an organized thought throughout the writing, and it is presented logically and with support.	Essay content is mostly strong, and there is often an organized thought in the writing. It is mostly logical and offers some support.	Essay content shows some effort made to provide an organized thought, but there are gaps in structure and content, and more support is needed.
Grammar and Punctuation _____/15 pts.	Essay has little to no grammatical or punctuation errors. Strong effort in editing and revising clearly evident.	Essay has some grammatical or punctuation errors, but effort is still evident.	Essay struggles with multiple grammatical or punctuation errors. More effort needed in editing and revising.
Word Choice _____/15 pts.	Essay reads well. Strong word choice and sentence variety.	Essay mostly reads well. Word choice is mostly strong, and there is some sentence variety.	Essay reads choppy and doesn't flow well. Better word choice needed.

Total: _____/50 pts.

Advanced Essay Rubric:

Grading Categories:	Excellence	Marked Competence	Basic Proficiency	Below grade - level proficiency	Inadequate for grade credit
Thesis Statement ____/pts.	Essay concentrates on a central idea and reveals a clear, sound organizational plan.	The essay has a clearly stated central, logically, and adequately developed thesis. Although it shows competence, the B paper lacks the originality, depth of thought, and mastery of style that characterizes the A paper.	Essay has a central idea expressed clearly enough to convey the essay's thesis to the reader. Organization, coherence, and unity of thought must be sustained in the essay as a whole.	States but fails to develop and sustain a central idea.	Fails to state a central idea
Organization ____/pts.	Essay follows proper format with a strong introduction, body, and conclusion. Essay follows essay guidelines with proper organization and format throughout.	Essay mostly follows proper format with a good introduction, body, and conclusion. Essay mostly follows essay guidelines with proper organization and format throughout. There are some organization errors, but they are minor.	Essay partly follows proper format with an introduction, body, and conclusion. Essay partly follows guidelines with some organization and some effort toward proper format. However, there are clear and/or specific organizational errors.	Essay lacks proper format with a missing or incomplete introduction, body, and/or conclusion paragraphs. The essay sometimes follows guidelines, but mostly does not.	Essay clearly lacks proper format. Adherence to essay guidelines were not met and/or followed.
Content ____/pts.	Essay's content is focused, in-depth, and rigorous in analysis, explanation, and/or argumentation. Paragraphs stay focused and support the thesis statement throughout.	Essay's content is mostly focused, in-depth, and mostly rigorous in analysis, explanation, and/or argumentation. Paragraphs mostly stay focused and support the thesis statement throughout.	Essay's content is sometimes focused and sometimes rigorous in analysis, explanation, and/or argumentation. Paragraphs partly stay focused and try	Essay lacks strong content throughout. There is a lack of focus or a lack of depth in paragraph topics and support. Paper sometimes supports thesis statement, but there is a lack of	Essay lacks adequate content. There is a lack of focus and a lack of understanding of essay guidelines and proper essay completion.

			to support the thesis statement.	substantial content.	Parts are missing or incomplete.
Vocabulary _____/pts.	Employs effective, appropriate words and phrases.	Employs effective, appropriate words and phrases.	Shows lack of depth in vocabulary and use of phrases.	Very limited use and/or inappropriate vocabulary	Inadequate or inappropriate use of vocabulary
Grammar _____/pts.	Makes careful use of transitional devices; maintains a consistent and appropriate tone; free from mechanical errors; Uses standard American English	Few or minor errors in the use of English	Avoids serious errors in the use of English, but lacks the vigor of expression or development of a B or A paper	Serious and/or numerous errors in use of grammar.	Inadequate or inappropriate use of grammar.
References _____/pts.	Clearly documents the ideas and writing of others in an acceptable format.	Clearly documents the ideas and writing of others in an acceptable manner.	Clearly documents the ideas and writing of others in an acceptable manner.	Fails to clearly document the ideas and writing of others in an acceptable format.	Fails to clearly document the ideas and writing of others in an acceptable manner.
Proofreading _____/pts.	Free from mechanical errors	Comparatively free from errors, shows evidence of having been spell checked and proof read	Paper has errors that would have been caught by word processor, spelling, and grammar checks	No signs of having been proofread.	No signs of having been proofread.

Total: _____/pts.

Thank you for your purchase!

Please consider these other valuable resources from Late November Learning Tree:

Journaling Is Writing Too!

Journaling Through Scriptures for Teens

Journaling for Kids

Poetry Practice

Paragraph Practice